WOVEN WORDS PUBLISHERS *Presents*

THIS LOVE OF MINE

Born and brought up in Kolkata, Soumi had started her career as an HR Recruiter. At present, she is pursuing Master's Degree in Psychology, while working as a Content Writer. Passionate about music, she is an occasional singer herself. Her literary works have been published in several web and little magazines. A collection of her Bengali poems was published in 2009, followed by A PEN IN THE MARSHES (2016), her first tryst with fiction. THIS LOVE OF MINE is the first collection of her English poems.

This
LOVE *Of* MINE

Soumi Dutta

Woven Words Publishers OPC Pvt. Ltd.
Registered Office:
Vill: Raipur, P.O: Raipur Paschimbar,
Dist: Purba Midnapore, Pin: 721401,
West Bengal, India.
www.wovenwordspublishers.net
Email: editor@wovenwordspublishers.net

First published by
Woven Words Publishers OPC Pvt. Ltd., 2017

ISBN-13: 978-81-934093-9-8
ISBN-10: 8193409396

Price: $8

Printed and bound in India

To "D"

STRIPPER

Some random lines – the way you make me feel

When I fear getting caught, trying to steal

Memories of yours – broken silky waves

Which define my aimless enclaves.

I want you as deep as dark circles of mine.

I want your disorder, had too much sunshine.

Semiprecious distractions enlighten my crevices.

As I continue to depend

On external devices, I hate to even name.

I do not have the ploy to hold your reality.

Indelible drunken episodes

Make me juxtapose bloodbaths and sororities.

My own impudence manhandles my coherence.

Losing my pride was not without misgivings.

Capacities send ultimatums.

Resolutions are seduced by stupefaction.

As I strip to go to bed, I strip with only one reason –

Just so I can beg for you again.

HEAP OF SOOT

That I am writing after a year

Tells me how much I love you.

No, I don't want to prove it,

I am happy that I can cry.

What I didn't know is that all this would happen.

I have incomplete and incoherent thoughts,

Little crazy scraps of loose emotions,

And a heap of soot on my lazy eyes.

HOLDING ON

Some questions, answers and some moments of silence

Had changed many things inside the little room.

A few seconds had changed lots and lots…

But was it, Me or you?

This was the big question then.

We do not solve everything every time,

We do not want to.

We are lazy when it comes to giving reasons,

What does one get

Holding on?

Your fists are so small…

How much is a human being?

YOUR DREAMS

Still your dreams in the nook of your room excite me,

Like an old toy

Belonging to someone else.

BALD

I just pick my pieces and give them away,

Pretending they are simply me after all,

I get white and red, but never black and blue,

Killing time so I will learn back how to crawl.

I try to look and eat, so happy just in case,

Want to fit in size 6 as well gain some weight.

I like the way I'm slimming (hate the glow it takes

Off my skin which needs a desperate disgrace).

I go on, bargain, play a fool, or try a hash,

I always have liked rules, never had a racy tilt,

Now I desire to train my kite some more,

I do not care enough to let my quest sink in.

They keep on saying I'm losing my hair

By the minute, also all of it's my fault.

ANOTHER ONE OF MY FLEETING NEEDS

If you really are mine,

I don't want to hurt you.

I have to take you out of this game.

You are late.

I cannot afford to be what I really am.

I can only hope that you too

Turn out to be just another one of

My fleeting needs, to fall in love again.

A WHIP

The unspent evenings look for solitude.

A whip, and this personal note ends with regrets, conscience.

MANHATER

A man

Is not enough to alter me?

Only the phone calls I make are turning insane,

And I lost my consistency,

For it resembled you.

And I am feeling cold,

Kind of like you.

Creativity, takes care of me,

At least for this untimely morning.

And I am feeling old, reluctance,

Kind of like me.

UNCIVILISED FEELINGS

Last night I had plunged, trying to be as hard as my intolerance,

With the acute need to forget about all the times I trembled,
ignoring the needles that talk into me,

Trying to erase all traces off my loot.

An extreme capitalist,

Manifesting and testing.

Each time I am more determined to have a showdown,

I relinquish the darkness of putting an end to your cigarettes.

I experience and tolerate you,

Get used to it all,

But living in a dream is better than having my brains fucked out

And I need to protect myself

As you need to breathe.

If you think I speak of nonsensical assumptions,

You might very well be right.

Last night, when I realised what was happening, I knew I had to be wooden.

Last night, amour, uncivilised feelings had forced in.

IMPLYING

I have been lying and you have been implying

One streak of grey hair,

One strand of something.

Floating word-drops

Are careless around you.

EXPECTATIONS

These do not mean love.

Just like you know when I am lying all the time.

Believe in my fear of losing you,

Understand.

I will stop,

Because you have expectations.

You expect me to know, you don't believe me

Anyway.

FRAIL FRAME

I wouldn't have worn the sweater if you hadn't asked me to.

Every time I wear my stole, I feel I get to copy my sister.

Peppered with certified copycat meows and demands,

Lie my worries about you.

Fragile.

Writing

Is a painful process for me?

Trying to keep this as personal as possible

(And now my hair has started copying your hair colour as well).

I cannot take profanities from you,

Now I miss you and I am afraid to tell you

The analysis of my association with coldness and winter.

Love is the blanket that would have kept me warm during the coldest of nights before,

But now when I am out alone, crying, I don't feel anything.

Once you reach,

I switch my location off.

Frail frame,

Pathetic with roads,

Scared and confused,

You get sick easily.

You have seen me at my worst.

In each other's purses,

I am a paper,

You are a clip.

SHE

She used to sit on this chair,

and stopped talking for reasons she wouldn't share,

She used to grace that corner,

No Ken needed to adorn her.

She used to see through my fake smile,

Making our silence worthwhile.

COMMON SALT

I am not waiting.

Anymore.

It's not because I am there.

But

Because I am there with you.

I like to see a love story in porn.

Salt, common salt in my ears.

VALENTINE'S DAY

You don't meet all my demands but

You have spoilt me.

We are not supposed to be too close.

But then I could tell you when I first fell in love with you.

I want to keep spending Sundays with you just like I am used to.

Why should it matter,

Jaywalker?

DIVINE BEAUTY

Prodding.

A list of us suffices.

Why do you go to the office?

Don't I know!

Offing.

A beach person.

Sequestered.

Divine beauty.

And all that she said.

MOSTLY OF SUNLIGHT

Afraid of the dark,

But mostly of sunlight.

Some say I am kind of quirky,

Some say, "Yeah, normalcy is overrated."

I malign you because it is the only way I get to talk about you.

Obscure?

I want it to be.

SUNDAY

Another Sunday with you.

Cats and dogs.

You are the last person I want to see

(They are creating an IV) –

Because you speak decent English,

But

English can be so cold.

"Sit properly", I say

Tucking your brastrap in.

I have started loving cats because of you.

I DO NOT OFFEND ANYMORE

I do not offend anymore.

Love is like getting down a rickshaw,

Mad like your belly button.

TAKE ME HOME

Inside the closet, I spread.

More.

In rotational dreams, I am gangraped

I am prostituted thrice.

The main reason for inheritance being late

Gets down behind the desk

Too generic.

What kind of kisser I am?

And how do I fornicate?

Will you not come to take me home from school?

ULTRASONIC

How many days have we not fought?

Step-sisterly behaviour!

You think I laugh at you.

You are angry when I don't know how to react,

When I smile

(Why would that even happen when it's you?)

Silly,

Digressing sensor.

Maybe that's how I want to think of you.

BUT

As if I had any other choice

When it came to

Your obsession regarding teaching me how to kiss –

If I knew you were making love to me for the last time

I would have felt somewhat warmer,

But you are not dead.

GRAPHIC

What I had looked for in you was graphic.

Are you here enough? At the tip of my hair?

Come sticking, all the way.

I got too serious. You have been busy.

CONFUSE ME

You cheated on yourself when you cared to use me,

Never liked me enough to want to refuse me,

You always cared very much though (so as to confuse me).

NAIL PAINT

I want no one to think I have a beautiful heart,

Whatever I may regret, I don't regret my friends.

Wherever I go,

I carry you in my chipped nail paint.

GET YOU CHOCOLATES AGAIN

You forgot my name for the first time today,

Let's take a walk again.

I was always afraid you would kick me away.

Do you know the difference between "I won't let you cry" and "I won't make you cry"?

After naming the painful love affair,

It is disastrous if I sleep on my own.

You tire me way more than an orgasm does.

I feel an acute discomfort,

But if I stop, I won't know what else to do.

I don't find any meaning to my poet's greed.

I lock your traces on my pages where I don't want to
acknowledge you at all,

To strip myself better.

Bitter taste –

All of it won't last till I reach my head.

A pseudo masochisticsuperlativity –

To see the paper and the pen copulate when every time I bleed
like a virgin.

How I used to hate open endings, relationships heading nowhere

You were an accident all the time,

A journey that I had dared to take.

Playing with the smoker I thought was just a little girl,

I try to write good things about you.

Every time I am not honest to myself,

I try to steal a little comfort.

Denying the inevitable in me,

I am magic.

And I can never get you chocolates again.

DOUBLE STANDARDS

You don't know, once I had been with a woman.

Think of what you'd think of me had you known.

Beyond double standards,

Knocking my fireplace down,

Everyone forgot there was an "us".

Hairline trauma –

No sleep can deter it.

No unconsciousness can make them fade away,

Lines that deserve to be written.

DOUBLE STANDARDS 2

Attending to the day run by her,

Chirping,

I bathe her. I say so many things against her,

I stop breathing.

Even if I cry in my solitude, I get ticketed.

I cannot decide.

Slant thoughts block my trust out,

Buries it in my hole with the thrust of my unable nails.

THE ONE

Should I feel empowered when you feel aloof?

Earlier I could have told you my dreams, the moment I'd wake
up from them.

Hour by hour, I wait for you.

"Aren't all of us broken?" you say.

But I'd never have thought I'd be broken because of you.

Your shell came between us.

But I have only one.

Yes, I have only one.

BURDENS

I have not loved the wrong people,

I have loved the wrong "you".

Burdens,

Not emoted anymore.

"It's probably not the right time," I had said.

NEED

Not so difficult to take anymore.

I skim through the contacts –

"Hey".

Reba to my Kelly,

My anhedonia,

I need to say, "I love you".

BIRDS IN A GRAVEYARD

And then I remember

The way she had held the little, white puppy at the pet fair,

The way she used to hit me in her sleep and cry in fear.

Every morning I find I have said to you in my dreams all that I
can't say to you anymore.

I have cried every time my mother died,

Jack Frost,

I wake up feeling so secure,

Thinking everything is all right again,

And then I remember birds in a graveyard.

GAY JOKES

Selfish – a name,

Suffering from misandry, I remain unsung.

"I fall in love with people," she had said,

Nowadays I laugh and crack gay jokes in class.

WISHFUL INTERPRETATIONS

It is easier to be cheated on than to cheat on you.

One thing.

I need one thing that proves you had come for me.

Drinking water at the middle of the night

That's the feat of intoxication I can achieve.

Why is it bad that I can't write?

Those

Wishful interpretations.

INTERRUPTIONS

Panties inside out,

Crying anew,

And I still want to hide

All the time,

All the time,

Do you think I am beautiful?

(I don't know because you don't tell me and it's fucking wrong!)

Interruptions are necessary,

Biological impulses...

PERFORMANCE

How had our conversation started?

I think of performance,

Even when I try to sleep.

Answer sheets ought to tell me

You have not gone anywhere.

Aimless,

For I want your time.

COLD

I have not walked the city streets with you.

When she takes your name,

I can smell dry winter,

And warm you.

Admitting to my imaginations, inertia,

I might see you while having a pedicure done.

With my very limited vocabulary –

May my face soften when I see you.

May my tears fall when I miss you.

May you know someday that I love you.

TROJAN HORSE

Trojan Horse,

This is not a way to live.

Your ring is on my cheek.

I read poetry that you gave me.

It is the only love story I acknowledge and which acknowledges
me.

I feel like dry ice - when you speak of Troy.

PANTS

Your form right by my shoulder

Takes care of all the complaints I have.

Five days I have walked with you.

You become the cloth covering my head.

You do not return my ring, neither do you wear it.

You take your hand away.

Nowhere to go

This is just what I had wanted.

Your head on my chest,

Your arms around my neck.

Caressing your footsteps,

I help you wear your socks.

A short, dark street.

You ask me what I want to say when my grip on you becomes
tighter.

On the fifth day, we go for a movie.

We go for lunch.

I pay the bill.

I give you ten bucks to give to the doorman who greeted us.

I have worn pants.

It makes me feel responsible for you even though theoretically I am against stereotypes.

I see you. I still cannot be your man.

A POET'S LOVE

I miss you.

Last night, I wanted to run to you, to hug you, like I have told you so many times. I was crying and had to gulp down my tears because I am not supposed to do otherwise. I am not supposed to be obsessed about you, I am not supposed to be in pain because of you. How can I cry for you? Why should I?

I miss the cold love you used to give me. Probably your brand of love was the right one. But then I don't know because now you have left me, just when I needed you the most. And you said you are not going anywhere, that you are right here.

I guess you did not have it in you to take a poet's love.

A HAPPY DAY

I say I am not looking for love. You tell me you do not care. But
I need to feel loved.

I do not want to sleep with you. Stay with me, stay beside me,
that is all I need.

Trying to earn myself back, I do everything to keep you out of
my mind. I do not know where I am heading. I do not know if I
am doing the right thing, if I am cheating on you. Why, oh why,
don't you even want to feel me?

Dream world. You do not want to get out of your dream world,
because you are an escapist. Nothing but an escapist.

You stun me. And when I try to confront you, you ask me to stop
involving you in everything.

I ask you what kind of talk that is. You ask me to find my kind
and go talk to them.

You block me. Facing you gets weird. You must have a plan?
How can I talk to you?

You explain your kind to me. You say you do not want me to
hand you my weak heart over. You ask me to stop letting you
hurt me. You say it is not fair for me at this point when I am not
ready to face the things happening around me.

I cannot stop myself from kissing you, for you are so complex. It
is a cycle. I cannot rely on you. You do not admit to have done
what you really did. But I cannot love anyone else.

Make me feel good. Put my head on your lap. Let me say, "I
want to say so much, but I can't." Comfort me.

You miss my friendship. Then you treat me so kind. I call you a wannabe, tell you it does not suit you.

You ask me if I will be awake till late at night. You call me an extreme romantic. I take you by surprise by trying to kiss your shoulders. The intensity with which you look at me, burns me. You are not pretty, you are so beautiful.

As we take a corner at the restaurant and make it our own, the staff comes to ask us how the food is. They are embarrassed to break the privacy of our scene. You are ashamed of them taking us for a couple. You tell me we are not. I ask you whose kisses you acknowledge even if you don't kiss them back. I ask you why. You have no answer.

Tell me you miss me. And it's a happy day for me.

THE NATURE OF OUR RELATIONSHIP

I can call you "my love", I can call you "my baby". I can tell you about my fears of losing you, even though I know you might be tired of it by now. I cannot stop myself. I am too afraid of not winning again.

You used to like my boyishness, the hair on my arms. You had said you would protect my wounded beast.

I had seen you. Confused. Those deep-set eyes. That tired voice. From when I used to practise kissing on my hand, it took me two years to understand.

Haven't you seen me struggling to touch my nose with yours? Haven't you noticed the way I hold doors open for you even if you don't like it?

Your embrace. The first time sitting opposite each other and having nothing to say. You couldn't even look at me. So, like you. I asked for your hand to hold. I said I never had one of my own.

Writing our initials on a stone, with lipstick. The heat between your fingers, when you put the nut in my mouth.

I wanted to shout your name out to everyone. But you couldn't let that happen. No one could know. Ever.

My feelings were not enough for you. I said I did not care if no one could know. I had never hidden my existence before, and now…. why did I even believe that you had fallen for me? Not believing would have been easier…

When we went out with friends, I stopped looking at you.

I welcomed your cigarettes. Last night you wanted to stay with me…finding their texts when I woke up in the middle of the night. My best friend, you did not say anything.

I was so broken. Every time I asked you why, you looked away. Every time you held my face against your neck.

I wanted to ravage you. I wanted to be an animal, but still I made love to you. Bathing your breasts with my salty kisses, I looked for inspiration.

You still cover my eyes when there's a violent scene on TV, but you tell me you do not love me the way I love you.

FANTASIZING ABOUT YOU

Here I am, without a care in the world, daydreaming and fantasizing about you. Those are the best moments I can steal out of my life.

You are my open secret. I am tired of hiding us.

My brothers keep asking, "Who's the lady?"

I am not happy but you are my life. As little as I get you, I feel I have gotten too much. You let me kiss you, but you do not kiss me back anymore. I go mad. As I kiss you, I want to shade you from the world. I want you to face nothing else again.

My hair on your face, makes me want to get rid of everyone coming between us. I will overcome all obstacles. You can post intimate pictures with anyone, you can go out with any boy you want, but you are mine.

I am jealous and protective. You are worth fighting for. I want to touch you. But the very thought of you makes me cry.

When I stand close to you, you become stiff. Oh! The twinkle in your eyes and the way you look at me from side. Do you want me? Did you want me ever?

It's out of my hands now.

I get red and I get wet as I realize I have been gyrating in my sleep, moving to your beats.

I love you.

YOUR MISTRESS

You make me feel like a boy, like a man; sometimes like a little girl, sometimes like a hungry, needy woman.

Waiting for you to caress me, I undress. Maddened with lust, I forget to switch the lights off.

Rejected by you again and again, where do I turn to? My imaginary lover!

I am waiting to be loved. No, there's no imaginary lover, no vagueness, it's all well-defined. It's you.

I am growing up, growing older. And you are not good for me. I am destroying myself, but I have never written better. The problem is, even if I go to someone else, you will not do or say anything.

I kiss you full on the lips, no fabric between us. Now is the time to love and to make memories. Soon both of us will be dragged into life's miseries and responsibilities. Then I cannot take you to the washroom anymore. I will be lying drunk and you running errands for your husband.

I want to use my brute force on you. I tried to be bad because I hate the way you make me feel. But make love to me because I love the way you make me feel.

Close, so close. Take yourself off. Do not say a word. I struggle to find your breasts on my mouth. I want to push you with my fingers and see what lies inside.

I am startled at the slightest noise when I am with you.

Do not pretend that whatever happened between us happened in my sleep. I cannot just forget it. Something really had happened.

Kiss me back before I wash my hands.

While I was exploring myself, I could not come out because I wanted it to happen when you were with me.

I want to taste you. I try to find your lips. Look at me. Then I kiss you more.

How many times have we been physical? How many times have I tried to express my insanity to you?

People ask me if you are using me for sex. They ask me about your sexuality, your gender. I do not want you to be less of a woman because you had once dared to say that you loved me too.

'I do not want you to love me. I do not want to love you.' I wish I could say those. But I just want to be your mistress.

THIS LOVE OF MINE

I demand too much. You do for me as much as you can. I really should not have anything else to ask of you.

I will never get you. Still I am so desperate to talk to you for a moment.

You say I do not talk sense anymore. The thing is, you do not want to listen to what I want to say, and the things you want to listen to, will not come out of me.

Should I try to treat you like a friend? I am not clear regarding how I can do that. If only I could tell myself that I never really loved anybody.

All the time, I want to say to you that 'I love you'. I am scared that if I do not, I will never be able to.

You say this love of mine is nothing compared to the love I had given you once. I had made you feel that I love you in all ways possible. I do not make you feel that way anymore. But when I hug you, hold you like I have nothing else to hold on to, and do not let you go, don't you feel anything?

I do not understand so much, I cannot analyse or think so much. I just know I love you. That's it. And I will always love you.

You are my existential crisis. I am trying to handle it but I don't know how to. I am not allowed to show it to anyone. At least do not push me away from you. I am so dependent on you. It is not healthy, but I have never been able to depend on anyone. Please do not leave me. I cannot see you with anyone else.

I surrender to you. Completely. I am begging on my knees.
Please do not go.

I do not want to stifle you. But I am in so much pain. I live with
so much insult.

Will you not take me?

LOVE LETTER

This is not the first love letter that I am writing to you. I write a love letter to you every day. You are not able to understand or read that. Or probably you do get it, but since things have changed now, you do not want to let me know.

You had asked me to write you two letters. One that you would be able to keep with you, another that you would not. But I can only write the one that you would not. You will not be able to keep a single letter I write to you, because when I write a letter to you, it is filled with love.

Some people have told me, they know I am a romantic when they read what I have written. Do you think so too?

I too want to get letters from you.

I had wanted this kind of love since I was a child, one that would romance me out of my wits. My love for you keeps haunting me.

Before today, I had not known how it felt to meet someone secretly. But I do not have the power to avoid your attraction.

But I got scared today, deeply. If anyone knows, all of it will be ruined. You will never forgive me. I am afraid to think about that day.

When you touched my hand today, I felt, "Who says she doesn't have feelings for me?"

After I confessed my feelings for you, I felt I belonged with you, to you. I had wanted someone, someone with whom to converse, I would not have to look for words.

I need to express our story desperately. That's why I write letters to you. I have only one person in this whole wide world to read my story.

SHE DOES NOT LOVE ME

If I come out, we will not be able to meet like we do anymore. I am turning into a monster fast and you are unsafe with me.

But you say nothing happens to you when I unclothe myself in front of you.

You had needed someone who'd smoke with you. None of my business though. I make everything my business but I forget that I could not matter less to you. You keep on telling me how irrelevant I am, but I do not ever get it.

Now you are incomplete, and I can only imagine myself as a beautiful woman; Not a man anymore. No attempts to allure you, but I am falling flat on my face. I want to have the right to be possessive about you.

When you had taken my blood, we had got stuck. This emptiness in my heart – I try to explain it to you without humiliating myself again and again. But you are never in the state of mind to listen to all that shit. I keep on saying that I love you, but nowadays I do not even get that silence back.

You "react" on my post stating I am in a complicated relationship. And I am addicted to my computer, typing away all my fatal thoughts about you.

"She does not love me, she does not care…"

MASTURBATING TO ANGELINA JOLIE

I lie on my single bed. You slither in, like a snake. My back hurts. I hide my face in my palms as I move away from you. I am angry with you. I am hurt. I want you to apologise. I want you to make it up to me, make things all right. I want you to plead with me, to force me to take you back. I have not forgotten your touch. That is why it haunts me still.

Crying, I invite you on top of me. I open myself for you. My legs hurt from the parting. Can you not see?

You keep hindering me while I try to explore my sexuality. Once again you throw me to the loneliness I have grown up with.

Even if I want to be someone's now, I cannot be. It does not feel right (anymore).

I draw a card for you. I use my left hand so that it contains the innocence absent in my right hand.

Your hair pins me down, blinds me, pierces me. Laziness now, vocals by Lana Del Rey…I lock my door like the first time I had locked it when I had you.

I cover my eyes. I wish I had electric blue eyes to hit you with. I am looking for a beautiful ending for myself.

My days are filled with Hungarian porn stars. I cannot fight with you over the girls we used to see on the streets.

I fall on my bed again. Masturbating to Angelina Jolie when I have trouble sleeping.

I unlock my door.

THE DISTANCE

If I write about you, it will be more difficult to forget you.

I will not get peace if I will not be able to forget you. At the same time, I believe I need a closure, like I have always needed. But I know I will not get a closure from you.

I have craved love and reassurance since forever. I do not know if you understand these needs of mine. I wanted to find momentary happiness with you. But I cannot love again. Not again.

Why did I feel today, when you hugged me, that you love me so so much? When you walk with me, why do you hold on to my sleeves?

I dream of you and I feel the red wine we had, going down my throat each time.

You are so indispensable to me. No one knows me better than you do. Is this distance only my fault? Only mine? Hadn't you tried to push me away?

I do not know how to deal with you. I do not feel safe with anyone else and my heart is not safe with you. You are the one I depend on to mend it. You are the one I am always afraid would break it. I cannot be with anyone else once I have known what it is like to be with you.

I am losing my mind.

BRUTAL FRIENDSHIP

Each morning used to bring a new hope to me, but as the day used to progress, I used to break my promise to myself of not thinking about you. I used to call you again, get insulted again and again. I used to say to myself, "One day I will stop calling you. One day I'll stop saying I love you."

I used to dread that day.

Hiding my tendencies, I used to go on. Used to ask you to spend nights with me, sleepless.

As I used to come on to you, you used to be ashamed of me, of yourself, of us.

One day I will forget your number. I will forget all you wanted was distance from me and at the same time you wanted to be friends. I will forget you had said, "Never stop talking to me."

I could not even tell you for one final time that you are the reason I am broken this way. You had sealed my lips with your brutal friendship.

www.ingramcontent.com/pod-product-compliance
Lightning Source LLC
Chambersburg PA
CBHW020605030426
42337CB00013B/1224